CHAKA THE SEQUOIA

POEMS AND ILLUSTRATIONS BY JUSTIN JEROME MITCHELL

NURTURE NATURE CULTURE PRESERVATION
NURTURE NATURE CULTURE PRESERVATION
NURTURE NATURE CULTURE PRESERVATION
NURTURE NATURE CULTURE PRESERVATION
NURTURE NATURE CULTURE PRESERVATION
NURTURE NATURE CULTURE PRESERVATION
NURTURE NATURE CULTURE PRESERVATION
NURTURE NATURE CULTURE PRESERVATION
NURTURE NATURE CULTURE PRESERVATION
NURTURE NATURE CULTURE PRESERVATION
NURTURE NATURE CULTURE PRESERVATION

ISBN: Softcover   978-1-7960-2170-7
          Hardcover   978-1-7960-2171-4
          EBook   978-1-7960-2169-1

Print information available on the last page

Rev. date: 03/21/2019

To order additional copies of this book, contact:
Xlibris
1-888-795-4274
www.Xlibris.com
Orders@Xlibris.com

ACKNOWLEDGEMENT
For my mother and Father,
I honor you always
and I am forever greatful.

From the heavens to the ground
Gods glory is seen all around
In Mother Nature life consists
Of sorts of creatures stupendous
A wonder in creations sight
In the unseen survivals might
Will be revealed in what remains
To seek a unique new domain
And through it all God is still good
Eternal refuge understood

PLACED IN THE LAND
TO OVERSEE
WAS CHAKA
THE SEQUOIA TREE
UPLIFTING NATURE
STURDY AND TALL
CHAKA INCREASED
THE MOST OF ALL

6

TWO SUNBIRDS CAME
DOWN FROM THE SKY
AND BUILT A HOME THERE
WAY UP HIGH
THEY LIVED WITH CHAKA
LONG BEFORE
THEY LEFT A NEST EGG
THERE WAS AURA

8

WAY DOWN LOW A
SPIDER LATCHED
ONTO CHAKA'S BARK

HEREAFTER
UP THE TREE
NOMADA CREPT
TO SEIZE SOMETHING
INSIDE HER WEB

10

SWIFT AND SLY

A DRAGONFLY

SWAYS AND BUZZES

CLOSE NEARBY

TO THE TOP

SOBORNO PRESSED

TO SEEK WHAT

WAS LEFT

IN CHAKA'S NEST

OTHER CREATURES SEE
THAT NEST TOO
THEY WANT THAT EGG
AND THINK IT'S FOOD
THE SHELTERED SUPPORT
THAT CHAKA GIVES
PROVIDES ALL THAT
THEY'LL NEED TO LIVE

14

UP THEY GO
UNTIL IT RAINS
ABOVE THE CLOUDS
AURA IS SAFE
LIGHTNING AND THUNDER
STRIKES BELOW
UP THERE NOW THEY
CANNOT GO

16

NOMADA'S WEB WAS
WASHED AWAY
SO SHE CAME BACK
ANOTHER DAY
SHE SLOWLY STARTS
TO CLIMB BACK UP
TO TRAP HER PREY
AURA CLOSE UP

18

SOBORNO SEES HER
SO SHE TRIES
TO FLY UP THERE
AND STEAL HER PRIZE

EACH PULLS THE OTHER
DOWN TO TAKE
THAT NEST EGG THAT
THEY DIDN'T MAKE
IF THIS CONTINUES
AT THIS RATE
THEY WON'T PROGRESS
THAT IS THEIR FATE

CHAKA'S AURA IS
SAFE FOR NOW
TOO FAR TO SCALE
THEY DON'T KNOW HOW

EACH TIME, THEY'VE TRIED
THIS WAY OR THAT
BUT THIS TIME
AS THEY RISE UP
THERE TO SNATCH
THE NEST EGG SHIFTS
AND STARTS TO HATCH

26

FIRST TO EMERGE
IS AURA'S FOOT INTACT

NEXT IS HIS WING

AND LAST A HEAD

AURA'S EYES OPEN
AND HE SEES
NOMADA CLIMBING
UP HIS TREE
THE WEB THAT SHE SPUN
HE SEES TOO
AND SOBORNO
AS SHE FLEW

NOW THAT AURA'S
OUT OF HIS SHELL
HE FLAPS HIS WINGS
TO FLY BUT FELL

32

DOWN HE DIVES
TOWARD THE FLOOR
AS HE FALLS
HE EATS SOBORNO

34

THE SPIDER LURKING
GRABS HIS LIMB
AND WRAPS A
TANGLED TRAP
FOR HIM

HE CHEWS HIS PREY
AND SHAKES HIS FOOT
TO FREE HIMSELF
FROM WHAT SHE PUT
A STICKY WEB THAT ALMOST
GOT HIM CAUGHT
BUT FIRST HE ATE NOMADA

HE ATE THE
DRAGONFLY AND SPIDER
THEN HE USED HIS
WINGS TO FLY

INTO THE SKY
TO JOIN HIS FLOCK
UNTIL HE COMES
BACK HOME TO CHAKA

NOW IN HIS NEST
THERE IS NO EGG
OR SPIDER TRAPS TO PULL HIS LEG
NO DRAGONFLIES
UP THERE TO PLOT
WHAT THEY CAN STEAL
OR WHAT HE'S GOT
ON CHAKA AURA'S ON THE TOP

Printed in the United States
By Bookmasters